11·70

HEALING REVEALED

Robert Holburn

ISBN: 0-9716449-0-X

Preface

"Father, In the name of Jesus, I ask you to open the hearts, the minds, and the spirits of those who read this book. Father, I pray that their understanding would be enlarged, and that they would be open to your word. Father, enable them to understand their birthright, and empower them to activate the authority and power you have placed within. Father, I pray that your healing anointing would flow, and that all who are in need of healing would receive what you have for them. I pray this in Jesus' name.

Amen."

Table Of Contents

Acknowledgements

My deepest appreciation to . . .

My wife, Sharon, my fragile gift from God, what would I do without you? I am truly blessed by having you in my life. Thank you for your prayerful support, and for your care and patience during the preparation of this book. I am so thankful to God for bringing us together and for ordaining our marriage in heaven.

Rev. Dr. Bruce Harcourt, my long-time spiritual mentor and friend. The Lord has used you greatly in my life. Over the years, your direction, encouragement and prayerful support have brought me to where I am today. I thank God for your obedience and for what you have done on my behalf.

Rev. David Sture for your assistance and encouragement to proceed with publication.

My Lord and God for the calling that You have placed on my life, and for the direction given to me by Your Holy Spirit during this project.

Introduction

I was born into a family that was cursed and afflicted with sickness and disease. As a young man, my father volunteered for the British Army at the outbreak of war with Germany in 1939. He spent the next six years in the field, in campaigns that took him from North Africa to Germany. The stress and rigours of war took a heavy toll on his health, causing long-term heart disease. After suffering through a lengthy series of heart attacks, my father went home to be with the Lord at the young age of 52 years.

As a child, my mother was diagnosed as having strep throat. Since back in the 1930's, the antibiotics that we have today were not available, her strep throat quickly became rheumatic fever. The rheumatic fever left her with a lifelong heart condition, which greatly influenced her lifestyle. As a young adult, she spent almost a year in a sanatorium where she was treated for tuberculosis. My mother's heart failed on her 76th birthday, and she went home to be with the Lord.

In 1946, my mother gave birth to her first son, my older brother who only lived a few hours, dying of toxaemia. When I arrived on the scene in 1947, the same medical complications were in place. The doctor told my mother that the prognosis for my survival was not good, and that it was touch and go as to whether I would survive. I thank God that He had other plans for my life.

As a child, I had every childhood disease going and then some. When I was seven, I contracted scarlet fever and spent a number of weeks quarantined in an I.D. (Infectious Diseases)

Hospital. When I was ten years of age. I had an inflamed appendix and was rushed into hospital for surgery. When my father came to visit me, he jokingly said that he wished he could climb in bed beside me because he needed the rest. Two days later, he had his first major heart attack and ended up in same hospital.

A couple of days after my father being admitted to hospital, my mother fell and injured her hip. Our convalescence became a family affair in the truest sense of the word. While recuperating at home after my surgery, I developed shingles, probably as a result of the stressful family situation. With my six weeks off for the surgery being extended by a further five weeks for the shingles, I missed a lot of school time that year.

When I was fifteen, I noticed that I had a small lump on my left arm. Over a period of three months, the lump got bigger until it was the size of a golf ball. It was early in 1963 when I consulted with a surgeon, who promptly removed a fatty tumour from my arm. Fortunately the subsequent biopsy determined that it was benign. Little did I know that there was more to come!

In 1969, at the young age of twenty-two years, I ventured forth from Scotland to live in the outskirts of Metropolitan Toronto, Canada. Early in 1971, I began to notice that I had many small lumps on my arms, legs, chest and back. Many of these lumps were painful to the touch, and they itched all the time. After consulting with a surgeon, I had a number of these small fatty tumours removed. Fortunately, once again the biopsy performed determined that they were benign.

Over the next six years, I went through a number of surgical procedures to remove twenty-eight tumours in total. For every tumour I had removed, it seemed that two more would appear. Needless to say, I became increasingly concerned about the long-term prognosis. I found myself asking the question, "What if I get one of these tumours where it is inoperable?"

By mid 1977, my medical condition was getting worse, and as if things weren't bad enough, my personal life was also in a shambles.

I do thank and praise God for the obedience of those who minister in the workplace. Where I worked, there was a beautiful Christian man by the name of Lorne MacBurnie. Lorne had been faithfully witnessing to me for almost two years. It was when I was at my lowest point, he invited me to go with him to Peoples Church in Toronto to see a short film and hear a guest speaker. It took two visits to Peoples Church before I allowed the Holy Spirit to minister healing to my life. When I got up to leave, I felt a hand pressing on my chest, almost like it was pushing me back. I turned around and made my way down to the front of the church where I met Jesus for the first time.

Lorne had also spoken to me about a Salvation Army Major who prayed for people and they were healed. The following Saturday we went to a prayer meeting in Ajax, where Major Bruce Harcourt anointed me with oil, laid hands on me and prayed for healing. Prior to attending this meeting, using a purple dye (gentian violet) supplied by my surgeon, I had marked all the tumours I could feel on my chest. From my neck to my waist, I had counted and marked forty-six tumours. The Tuesday after being prayed over, I had an appointment with my surgeon to review what tumours would be removed at the next surgery. Of the forty-six tumours marked, all were gone except three. Surgery was cancelled, Hallelujah!

The word of God says that we are his workmanship, created to do good works according to His plan and purpose, Ephesians 2:10. I now know that God had a calling and a purpose for my life and Satan did not want that to become a reality. Even before my birth, Satan had attacked the health of both my parents, and even took the life of my older brother. After I was born, Satan attacked my health with the intent of removing me from the calling that God has for my life. A few weeks after I received healing, I had a prophetic word spoken over me that told me that I would teach the word. Obviously at that particular time in my spiritual life I had no concept of what God had planned for me. It wasn't until I had accumulated some life experiences, worked through some trials and tribulations, that God ordained me to become a minister of the Gospel.

On completion of my studies in 1998, I was ordained as a

Minister of the Gospel of Jesus Christ. At my ordination, God told me that He has called me to a Fivefold Ministry, with a specific anointing to teach and to pray for the healing of the sick. This book is the result of preparing a teaching on healing, a teaching that I have been instructed to present to His Church. It is God's desire that all of His people should not only walk in divine health, but if and when necessary, also have the knowledge of divine healing.

Yours in Him,

Robert (Bob) Holburn

Chapter 1

Divine Health Lost

In order to fully understand the concept of divine health and divine healing, we must go back to the beginning, to the very moment of creation, when God made all things. In the book of Genesis, Chapter 1, we are told that everything that God made was good. In the very last verse of the chapter, we are told that it was not just good, but "very good." In plain English, what God made had the right or required qualities; what He made was more than adequate, it was appropriate, it was complete, and of great worth. So it is, that when God created man, He created a physical being that was right, sound, and completely whole in every way.

Having been created right, sound, and completely whole, Adam and Eve then walked in divine health, which means that they never experienced any pain, sickness or disease. God created them this way because it was His will, meaning that it was His pleasure.

Revelation 4:11
11 "You are worthy, our Lord and God, to receive glory and honor and power, for you created all things, and by your will they were created and have their being."

We are all His people. Adam and Eve, you and I, we were all formed and made, created by God for His glory.

> *Isaiah 43:7*
> *7 everyone who is called by my name, whom I created for my glory, whom I formed and made."*

We are all God' workmanship, created to do good works, to fulfill His plan and His purpose.

> *Ephesians 2:10*
> *10 For we are God's workmanship, created in Christ Jesus to do good works, which God prepared in advance for us to do.*

In Genesis 1:27, we read that God made man in His own image. When we use the word image, we are usually referring to a photograph or a representation of an object. Therefore, by definition, the word image generally means the "imitation of an objects external form".

From Strong's #6754, "image" is tselem (tseh'-lem); from an unused root meaning to shade; a phantom, i.e. (figuratively) illusion, resemblance; hence, a representative figure, especially an idol: KJV-- image, vain shew. (DIC)

From the meanings of the words, shade, phantom, illusion, resemblance, we can extrapolate that physical man serves as a portrayal or symbol of God. Physical man, while bearing a likeness and similarity to God, is only a shadow of the real thing.

> *Genesis 1:27*
> *27 So God created man in his own image, in the image of God he created him; male and female he created them.*

Even though man was made in the image of God, and had been given rule over all of creation, he was given specific instructions regarding what he could eat from in the garden. Man was not allowed to eat from the tree of the knowledge of good and evil, and man (Adam) was warned that if he did this that he would die.

> **Genesis 2:16-17**
> **16 And the LORD God commanded the man, "You are free to eat from any tree in the garden;**
> **17 but you must not eat from the tree of the knowledge of good and evil, for when you eat of it you will surely die."**

As long as Adam and Eve were in perfect communion with God, they were in no danger of spiritual death. Neither were they in any danger of experiencing any physical sickness, disease, ageing or physical death. They walked in the divine health that God had provided for them. Even today, in this day and age, the degree of ability that we have to walk in divine health or to be healed, is directly proportional to our level of communion with God.

When Satan in the guise of a serpent, deceived the woman, Eve knew what trees that she and Adam were allowed to eat from. Conversely, she also knew which trees they were not allowed to eat from. The scripture in Genesis 3:3, details what God said to Adam and Eve, "You must not eat fruit from the tree that is in the middle of the garden, and you must not touch it, or you will die."

> **Genesis 3:1-3**
> **1 Now the serpent was more crafty than any of the wild animals the LORD God had made. He said to the woman, "Did God really say, 'You must not eat from any tree in the garden'?"**
> **2 The woman said to the serpent, "We may eat fruit from the trees in the garden,**
> **3 but God did say, 'You must not eat fruit from the tree that is in the middle of the garden, and you must not touch it, or you will die.'"**

Satan told Eve "You will not surely die," God will not kill you because when your eyes are opened you will be just like Him. Satan's statement to Eve was a blatant denial of one of God's divine

15

pronouncements, which was that if you eat you die! Eve chose to rise up in rebellion to God's command, and Adam, well he chose to follow suite. In their search for a measure of discernment and moral independence from God, both Eve and Adam ate from the tree of the knowledge of good and evil.

When God discovered that Eve, and then Adam had succumbed to the wiles of the enemy, He was quite explicit in describing what the consequences of their actions would be.

> *Genesis 3:16-17*
> *16 To the woman he said, "I will greatly increase your pains in childbearing; with pain you will give birth to children. Your desire will be for your husband, and he will rule over you."*
> *17 To Adam he said, "Because you listened to your wife and ate from the tree about which I commanded you, `You must not eat of it,' "Cursed is the ground because of you; through painful toil you will eat of it all the days of your life.*

Because He is a Holy God and cannot look upon sin, God then removes Adam and Eve from the garden. They were removed not just because of what they had done, but also for what they might become. The scripture in Genesis 3:22 states that man has now become like God. Having partaken of the tree of the knowledge of good and evil, Adam and Eve had acquired the same moral knowledge that God had. Since they had proved quite incapable of following God's command, what was to stop him from breaking yet another? If God had allowed them to stay, they would have been able to partake of the tree of life, which would have enabled them to live forever.

> *Genesis 3:22*
> *22 And the LORD God said, "The man has now become like one of us, knowing good and evil. He must not be allowed to reach out his hand and take also from the tree of life and eat, and*

live forever. "

It is still this way today; the knowledge of what is right and what is wrong does not provide the way to salvation, which leads to everlasting life. Sin was the root cause of Adam and Eve being removed from the garden. Sin caused their removal from divine health, and brought immediate spiritual death, physical pain, sickness, disease and finally physical death.

Through Satan's deception and man's sin, Satan became the Prince, Ruler and God of this world. Everything then came under his jurisdiction; his policy of sickness, disease, oppression, depression etc. became the reality for mankind.

Sadly, even in the body of Christ, the Church, many believers do not walk in divine health. Many have allowed sin in it's many forms to rob them of their divine health or their divine healing.

Chapter 2

Healing In The Old Testament

The consequence of the rebellion and sin of man is the loss of personal relationship with the Father. This loss of relationship with the Father, brought about mans spiritual death as well as his removal from divine health. On being removed from the garden, man was destined to suffer pain, sickness, disease, and finally physical death.

In spite of man's rebellion and sin, God has provided divine healing as a means of alleviating man's suffering. God knew that man, having the knowledge of good and evil, would not be able to live a sinless life. And so He initiated a new plan, a plan that provides a conditional avenue of relief from pain, sickness and disease, and sometimes even physical death itself.

Prior to what we refer to as the Covenant of Healing as detailed in Exodus 15:26, the only record of divine healing is that of Abimelech, King of Gerar, and his household. Abraham had moved into the region of Negev, and stayed in the city of Gerar for a while. It was the custom in those days for the King of the region to have his choice of the women. If a married woman caught the eye of the

King, it was not uncommon for the husband of the woman to disappear, or die under mysterious circumstances.

Sarah had caught the eye of Abimelech, and Abraham in fear of his life had lied to him. He told Abimalech that his wife Sarah was actually his sister. Believing that Sarah was Abraham's sister, Abimalech sent for Sarah, with the intent of adding her to his concubine. It was this action by Abimelech that prompted God to close up every womb in his household. Since Sarah was the to be the mother of the promised offspring to Abraham, God now intervened to obtain her release. God came to Abimalech in a dream and spoke to him.

> **Genesis 20:3-7**
> **3 But God came to Abimelech in a dream one night and said to him, "You are as good as dead because of the woman you have taken; she is a married woman."**
> **4 Now Abimelech had not gone near her, so he said, "Lord, will you destroy an innocent nation?**
> **5 Did he not say to me, 'She is my sister,' and didn't she also say, 'He is my brother'? I have done this with a clear conscience and clean hands."**
> **6 Then God said to him in the dream, "Yes, I know you did this with a clear conscience, and so I have kept you from sinning against me. That is why I did not let you touch her.**
> **7 Now return the man's wife, for he is a prophet, and he will pray for you and you will live. But if you do not return her, you may be sure that you and all yours will die."**

Abimelech responded very quickly to God's warning and called Abraham in to talk to him. He confronted Abraham and asked him why he had put him and his household in such jeopardy. Abraham explained his fear of being killed, and attempted to justify his actions by explaining to Abimelech that he and Sarah were born of the same mother but had different fathers. Sarah was returned to

Abraham, and in accordance with the instructions given in the dream, Abraham prayed for the healing of Abimelech and his household. God honoured His word and healed them all.

> **Genesis 20:17-18**
> **17 Then Abraham prayed to God, and God healed Abimelech, his wife and his slave girls so they could have children again,**
> **18 for the LORD had closed up every womb in Abimelech's household because of Abraham's wife Sarah.**

God had obviously made provision for divine healing prior to the covenant of healing coming into existence. We are truly fortunate that our God is a God of mercy and that He hears those who call on His name. In Exodus 3:7, we read that God heard the cries of the people of Israel who were suffering greatly under their Egyptian taskmasters. The scriptures tell us that when Moses brought the people of Israel out of Egypt, none of them were sick in any way. In order for this to be the case, God must have healed every single individual, male, female, young and old. We know that all were healed and walking in divine health, because the scriptures tell us that "no one faltered."

> **Psalm 105:37**
> **37 He brought out Israel, laden with silver and gold, and from among their tribes no one faltered.**

Having brought His people out of Egypt in divine health, God now sets the stage for the presentation of His covenant of healing. The people of Israel, some two million of them, have been travelling in the desert for three days and have not found any water. Our God has a most unique way of both preparing, and getting the attention of those with whom He wishes to communicate with, or send a message to.

So here we are, the stage is set, two million people are in the middle of the desert with no water to drink. One can only imagine what was going through the minds of the people. They were probably asking each other why God would bring them out of Egypt to let them die of thirst in the desert. When they did find water at Marah, they could not drink it because it was bitter. Suddenly, **fear set in, and does what fear does best, it destroys faith.** The people became agitated and spoke out against Moses, to the degree that even he was concerned for his life. Moses cried out to the Lord, who instructed him to throw a piece of wood into the water, and the water became sweet.

Now that He had everyone's attention, God delivers to His people what might be better defined as His covenant of health.

> *Exodus 15:22-26*
> *22 Then Moses led Israel from the Red Sea and they went into the Desert of Shur. For three days they traveled in the desert without finding water.*
> *23 When they came to Marah, they could not drink its water because it was bitter. (That is why the place is called Marah.)*
> *24 So the people grumbled against Moses, saying, "What are we to drink?"*
> *25 Then Moses cried out to the LORD, and the LORD showed him a piece of wood. He threw it into the water, and the water became sweet. There the LORD made a decree and a law for them, and there he tested them.*
> *26 He said, "If you listen carefully to the voice of the LORD your God and do what is right in his eyes, if you pay attention to his commands and keep all his decrees, I will not bring on you any of the diseases I brought on the Egyptians, for I am the LORD, who heals you."*

God's covenant of healing is **conditional,** and the four conditions that are detailed in verse 26, are as follows: -

1. **Listen carefully to the voice of the Lord your God.**
2. **Do what is right in His eyes.**

3. **Pay attention to all His commands.**
4. **Keep all His decrees.**

Divine health is undoubtedly God's plan for His people. His covenant of healing was not specifically given the people of Israel as an insurance policy against sickness and disease. The scripture states that if all four conditions were met, God would not bring any of the diseases on them that He brought on the Egyptians. The message is given loud and clear, that those who are obedient to God's word will not become sick. The latter part of verse 26 says, "for I am the LORD, who heals you." which literally means, *"I am the LORD who maintains your divine health."*

The people of Israel were under the law, and as long as they remained within the law, God maintained their health. If they disobeyed the law, the result was that they were removed from God's protection. God is not the author of sickness and disease; only Satan has full rights to that title. What God did was this: -

1. **As long as the people of Israel complied with His covenant He maintained their health.**
2. **As soon as they broke covenant He removed His protection.**
3. **Satan was then allowed to implement his policy of sickness and disease.**

God even goes one step further and states in Deuteronomy 7:15, that He will keep His people free from every disease and will inflict them on those who hate His people. God is clearly stating here that divine health is a blessing and sickness and disease are a curse.

> *Deuteronomy 7:15*
> *15 The LORD will keep you free from every disease. He will not inflict on you the horrible diseases you knew in Egypt, but he will inflict them on all who hate you.*

To reinforce the gravity of being obedient to His will, God lists the various diseases that will be a result of disobedience in

23

Deuteronomy 28. All are identified as curses.

> *Deuteronomy 28:15*
> *15 However, if you do not obey the LORD your*
> *God and do not carefully follow all his commands*
> *and decrees I am giving you today, all these*
> *curses will come upon you and overtake you:*

- In verse 22 we have consumption, fever and inflammation.

> *Deuteronomy 28:22*
> *22 The LORD will strike you with wasting*
> *disease, with fever and inflammation, with*
> *scorching heat and drought, with blight and*
> *mildew, which will plague you until you perish.*

- In verse 24 we have plague

> *Deuteronomy 28:24*
> *24 The LORD will turn the rain of your country*
> *into dust and powder; it will come down from the*
> *skies until you are destroyed.*

- In verse 27 we have boils, tumours and itch.

> *Deuteronomy 28:27*
> *27 The LORD will afflict you with the boils of*
> *Egypt and with tumors, festering sores and the*
> *itch, from which you cannot be cured.*

- In verse 28 we have madness, blindness and confusion of mind.

> *Deuteronomy 28:28*
> *28 The LORD will afflict you with madness,*
> *blindness and confusion of mind.*

- As if this wasn't enough to get the attention of the people of Israel, God makes His position clear in verses 60 and 61. He says to the people of Israel, that if they were not obedient, He will bring the dreaded diseases of Egypt along with every kind of sickness and disaster, until they were obliterated.

Deuteronomy 28:60-61
60 He will bring upon you all the diseases of Egypt that you dreaded, and they will cling to you.
61 The LORD will also bring on you every kind of sickness and disaster not recorded in this Book of the Law, until you are destroyed.

It is obvious from all the scriptures quoted that sickness is a curse and that divine health and divine healing are a blessing. In the Old Testament, the law was quite explicit when referring to what would happen if we were disobedient to God. It should not come as a surprise to we believers, why so many people are sick today. How many people do you know, friends, family, neighbours, workmates, who are walking in some form of sin or disobedience?

Remember what Jesus said in Matthew 5:17, He said that He had not come to abolish the Law and the Prophets but to fulfill them.

Chapter 3

Relationship With The Father

If we have are to have a relationship with the Father, it is absolutely necessary that we communicate with Him. As a marriage counsellor, I am always telling couples how important it is for them to maintain communications. As a counsellor, I have seen many marriages fail because of a lack of communication. As a pastor I have also seen many spiritual relationships fail from the same cause.

We need to communicate with Him, we need to talk to our heavenly Father. He cannot hear our prayers if we do not speak to Him. God loves us so much because He created us to have fellowship with Him. The scripture in James 4:5, tells us that God is a jealous God, He jealously longs for our faithfulness and love.

James 4:5
5 Or do you think Scripture says without reason that the spirit he caused to live in us envies intensely?

Just as sin broke Adam and Eve's communion with God, sin will prevent or break our communion with God. It was the sinless life of Jesus that enabled His relationship with the Father, and it was certainly the key that opened up His miraculous ministry. His ability to hear what God was saying, and to see what God was doing, was the result of His intimacy with the Father.

If we desire to walk in a miraculous ministry, we will be required to develop a Jesus kind of relationship. It is a child-like relationship based on intimacy and obedience that provides access to God's power. To fully understand the level of communion that Jesus had with the Father, we need to go back to the beginning: -

- Jesus' relationship with God was from the beginning. As an integral part of the Trinity, Jesus was there at the very moment of creation. It seems quite appropriate to envisage the Father, the Son, and the Holy Spirit, in consultation over what to make next, and how to make it.

John 1:1
1 In the beginning was the Word, and the Word was with God, and the Word was God.

- Jesus, in obedience to the Father, not only became flesh, but also lived a sinless life. He came to fulfill scripture, to fulfill God's promise, and to demonstrate God's glory to mankind. .

John 1:14
14 The Word became flesh and made his dwelling among us. We have seen his glory, the glory of the One and Only, who came from the Father, full of grace and truth.

- Jesus knew the Father intimately. The depth of His relationship with the Father was beyond measure. He had been with the Father in heaven, and He spoke only about the things that He knew. The inference here is that everything Jesus knew, flowed out from His experience with the Father.

John 3:11-13
11 I tell you the truth, we speak of what we know, and we testify to what we have seen, but still you people do not accept our testimony.

*12 I have spoken to you of earthly things and you
do not believe; how then will you believe if I
speak of heavenly things?*
*13 No one has ever gone into heaven except the
one who came from heaven-- the Son of Man.*

- Jesus, having been sent by God, speaks the words of God,
  and has the Spirit without limit. This confirms that every
  word that comes out of the mouth of Jesus, is God ordained,
  God authorized and God approved. Having come from the
  Father, Jesus taught from divine experience, and the result of
  this was that He walked in a God powered anointing.

John 3:32-34
*32 He testifies to what he has seen and heard, but
no one accepts his testimony.*
*33 The man who has accepted it has certified that
God is truthful.*
*34 For the one whom God has sent speaks the
words of God, for God gives the Spirit without
limit.*

- Jesus said that His father was always at work and that He
  works with the Father. They were a team where Jesus took
  direction from the Father. His relationship with the Father
  did not allow Him to do anything on His own initiative.

John 5:17
*17 Jesus said to them, "My Father is always at his
work to this very day, and I, too, am working."*

- Because of the love that the Father has for the Son, the
  Father shows the Son everything. Jesus said that He could do
  nothing on His own, that He took direction from His Father.
  In simplistic terms, what Jesus heard and saw the Father do in
  the spiritual realm, He caused to be spoken and manifested
  into existence in the physical realm. It was the depth of their
  relationship that enabled this to become a reality.

John 5:19-21
19 Jesus gave them this answer: "I tell you the truth, the Son can do nothing by himself; he can do only what he sees his Father doing, because whatever the Father does the Son also does.
20 For the Father loves the Son and shows him all he does. Yes, to your amazement he will show him even greater things than these.
21 For just as the Father raises the dead and gives them life, even so the Son gives life to whom he is pleased to give it.

- Jesus does God's will to bring honour to the Father. He states that what He speaks is not from Himself but from His Father who sent Him. We can only prove the validity of what He speaks by choosing to do God's will for our lives.

John 7:16-18
16 Jesus answered, "My teaching is not my own. It comes from him who sent me.
17 If anyone chooses to do God's will, he will find out whether my teaching comes from God or whether I speak on my own.
18 He who speaks on his own does so to gain honor for himself, but he who works for the honor of the one who sent him is a man of truth; there is nothing false about him.

- Jesus does nothing on His own and He only speaks what the Father has taught Him. He and the Father are communicating one with the other constantly, and this is so because Jesus does what pleases the Father.

John 8:28-29
28 So Jesus said, "When you have lifted up the Son of Man, then you will know that I am and that I do nothing on my own but speak just what the Father has taught me.

29 The one who sent me is with me; he has not left me alone, for I always do what pleases him

- Jesus and the Father are one, and the miracles He performed were proof of His relationship with the Father.

John 10:30
30 I and the Father are one."

- The scripture in John 14:20 adds to this scripture written in John 10:38, where Jesus says that, "I am in my Father, and you are in me, and I am in you." Thank you Lord for working miracles through those who have Jesus in them.

John 10:37-38
37 Do not believe me unless I do what my Father does.
38 But if I do it, even though you do not believe me, believe the miracles, that you may know and understand that the Father is in me, and I in the Father."

- Jesus exemplified the Father by speaking and doing the Father's work. His intimate relationship with the Father enabled Him to imitate or model the very nature of the Father. In other words, when you see Jesus you see the Father.

John 14:10-11
10 Don't you believe that I am in the Father, and that the Father is in me? The words I say to you are not just my own. Rather, it is the Father, living in me, who is doing his work.
11 Believe me when I say that I am in the Father and the Father is in me; or at least believe on the evidence of the miracles themselves.

- Jesus states that if we are in relationship with Him, He will work through us to bring glory to the Father. We are to ask in

31

His name and He will ask the Father to do it. We have the right and authority to do this based on His relationship to the Father.

John 14:12-14
12 I tell you the truth, anyone who has faith in me will do what I have been doing. He will do even greater things than these, because I am going to the Father.
13 And I will do whatever you ask in my name, so that the Son may bring glory to the Father.
14 You may ask me for anything in my name, and I will do it.

- Jesus says that if we love Him, we will do as He asks. If we do as He asks, He will ask the Father to send us another counsellor, the Holy Spirit to be with us, to live in us forever.

John 14:15-17
15 "If you love me, you will obey what I command.
16 And I will ask the Father, and he will give you another Counselor to be with you forever—
17 the Spirit of truth. The world cannot accept him, because it neither sees him nor knows him. But you know him, for he lives with you and will be in you.

- The relationship that we have with Jesus is forever. We who believe and are saved will be spending eternity with Him. While we are still doing His work on earth we will never be abandoned, through the Father, He has sent us the Holy Spirit to take His place.

John 14:18
18 I will not leave you as orphans; I will come to you.

- Because of our relationship with Jesus, we will understand His relationship to the Father. It is this relationship that enables the Father, through the Son, through the Holy Spirit, to manifest His works through us.

John 14:19-21
19 Before long, the world will not see me anymore, but you will see me. Because I live, you also will live.
20 On that day you will realize that I am in my Father, and you are in me, and I am in you
21 Whoever has my commands and obeys them, he is the one who loves me. He who loves me will be loved by my Father, and I too will love him and show myself to him.

- Jesus has now gone to be seated at the right hand of the Father to make intercession for us. He has passed the torch onto us and we are to continue His work, which is the work of the Father, here on earth.

John 20:21
21 Again Jesus said, "Peace be with you! As the Father has sent me, I am sending you."

These scriptures from the Gospel of John, the very words of Jesus, provide us with many of the important reasons why we must maintain a relationship with the Father. If we are to maintain divine health, and if required have access to divine healing, it is imperative that we are continually in communion, in relationship, with the Father.

Chapter 4

Healing Ministry Of Jesus

In His three years of ministry, Jesus healed countless numbers of people. During His ministry, there was such an outpouring of God's mercy and grace, which made everything that had come before appear insignificant. There are over forty occurrences of healing recorded in the four Gospels, and many of the accounts detail the healings of large numbers of people. The occurrences that are recorded in scripture, are no doubt the more dramatic instances, and by no means represent the totality of His healing ministry.

Jesus said that He had come not to destroy the Law and the Prophets, but to fulfil them. The Old Testament concept of sickness being the result of sin, and health and healing being the outcome of obedience, is still in effect. The coming of Jesus brought a greater revelation of God's plan of healing and Salvation for mankind. In reconciling man to God, Jesus enables the full force of the Trinity to come against and overcome sin, sickness, disease, physical death, and Satan himself.

Ephesians 6:12
12 For our struggle is not against flesh and blood,
but against the rulers, against the authorities,
against the powers of this dark world and against
the spiritual forces of evil in the heavenly realms.

The ministry of Jesus was inclusive of teaching His disciples how to do what he did. He established a format or methodology for the church, which has been passed down, to teach you and I how to access and activate the healing anointing of the Holy Spirit.

The methodology of His ministry was so radically different from what had been before, because Jesus had the first Fivefold Ministry. Jesus basically did it all, operating in all the offices of the Fivefold Ministry according to the needs of the situation. Paul in his letter to the Ephesians sums up the totality of the Ministry of Jesus. Apostle, Prophet, Evangelist, Pastor and Teacher, Jesus walked in all of these offices at one time or another.

Ephesians 4:11
11 It was he who gave some to be apostles, some
to be prophets, some to be evangelists, and some
to be pastors and teachers,

So great was the scope of His ministry that it was impossible for everything that He did to be documented. What has been recorded is a mere fraction of what actually took place. The occurrences that have been recorded have been deemed sufficient to help activate our faith to believe in the Christ.

John 20:30-31
30 Jesus did many other miraculous signs in the
presence of his disciples, which are not recorded
in this book.
31 But these are written that you may believe that
Jesus is the Christ, the Son of God, and that by
believing you may have life in his name.

The healing ministry of Jesus began after John the Baptist

baptized him in the river Jordan. Jesus was praying, He was in communion with His Father, when the Holy Spirit came on Him in the form of a dove. God acknowledged Him as His son, while others only considered Him as the son of Joseph, son of Heli. He was thirty years of age when His ministry began.

Luke 3:21-23
21 When all the people were being baptized, Jesus was baptized too. And as he was praying, heaven was opened
22 and the Holy Spirit descended on him in bodily form like a dove. And a voice came from heaven: "You are my Son, whom I love; with you I am well pleased."
23 Now Jesus himself was about thirty years old when he began his ministry. He was the son, so it was thought, of Joseph, the son of Heli,

- **What Motivated His Actions?**

Much of Jesus' ministry was motivated by His compassion for the sick, the dead and the dying. He saw the crowds of people as helpless lost sheep, not knowing what to do or where to go.

Matthew 9:36
36 When he saw the crowds, he had compassion on them, because they were harassed and helpless, like sheep without a shepherd.

As Jesus and His disciples were leaving Jericho, two blind called on Him to have mercy on them. They told Jesus that they wanted their sight restored. Jesus had compassion on them, and He restored their sight.

Matthew 20:34
34 Jesus had compassion on them and touched their eyes. Immediately they received their sight and followed him.

The presence of a strong faith always stimulated Jesus' desire to move. The centurion, whose servant was sick, had faith to believe that Jesus just had to say the word, and his servant would be healed. Jesus was so impressed with the faith of the centurion that He stated that he knew of no one in Israel with greater faith. This was quite a statement to make when you consider that the centurion was a soldier of Rome, part of the army of occupation.

> *Matthew 8:6-13*
> *6 "Lord," he said, "my servant lies at home paralyzed and in terrible suffering."*
> *7 Jesus said to him, "I will go and heal him."*
> *8 The centurion replied, "Lord, I do not deserve to have you come under my roof. But just say the word, and my servant will be healed.*
> *9 For I myself am a man under authority, with soldiers under me. I tell this one, `Go,' and he goes; and that one, `Come,' and he comes. I say to my servant, `Do this,' and he does it."*
> *10 When Jesus heard this, he was astonished and said to those following him, "I tell you the truth, I have not found anyone in Israel with such great faith.*
> *11 I say to you that many will come from the east and the west, and will take their places at the feast with Abraham, Isaac and Jacob in the kingdom of heaven.*
> *12 But the subjects of the kingdom will be thrown outside, into the darkness, where there will be weeping and gnashing of teeth."*
> *13 Then Jesus said to the centurion, "Go! It will be done just as you believed it would." And his servant was healed at that very hour.*

Jesus was also moved by the faith of the men who carried the paralytic to Him. The fact that He did not say, "you are healed", but said, "your sins are forgiven," was for the benefit of the teachers of the law. He did this to show them that He had the authority to forgive sins on earth. After explaining Himself, Jesus told the paralytic to get up, take his mat and go home.

Matthew 9:2
2 Some men brought to him a paralytic, lying on a mat. When Jesus saw their faith, he said to the paralytic, "Take heart, son; your sins are forgiven."

Jesus was certainly motivated to heal based on His own belief. Unfortunately, He was often limited by the unbelief of others. When He was in Nazareth, He could not perform any miracles because they did not have any faith in Him. To the people of Nazareth, Jesus was still the son of Joseph the carpenter. Fortunately, there were also times, when the presence and the power of the Holy Spirit were so evident, so ready to move and to heal.

Luke 5:17
17 One day as he was teaching, Pharisees and teachers of the law, who had come from every village of Galilee and from Judea and Jerusalem, were sitting there. And the power of the Lord was present for him to heal the sick.

- **Where Did He Heal?**

The healing ministry of Jesus was certainly a public ministry. All through the Gospels we read of Him ministering to large numbers of people out in the open. It is also true that from time to time, He was forced to heal privately. This was always a direct result of unbelief, and the negative atmosphere that unbelief generates. Before Jesus healed the daughter of Jairus, He first removed all the mourners from the room. He allowed only those to stay, who had complete faith and a total desire to see the young girl restored to life.

Mark 5:39-42
39 He went in and said to them, "Why all this commotion and wailing? The child is not dead but asleep."
40 But they laughed at him. After he put them all

39

out, he took the child's father and mother and the
disciples who were with him, and went in where
the child was.
41 He took her by the hand and said to her,
"Talitha koum!" (which means, "Little girl, I say
to you, get up!").
42 Immediately the girl stood up and walked
around (she was twelve years old). At this they
were completely astonished.

- **How Did He Heal?**

When Jesus ministered healing, He did not have a standard format or procedure. There was no healing ritual, only a response to the leading of His Father. As you have previously read, Jesus only said what He heard the Father say, and only did what he saw the Father do. There were times when He healed by physical contact, by merely **touching** the individual, just as He did with Peter's mother-in-law.

Matthew 8:15
15 He touched her hand and the fever left her,
and she got up and began to wait on him.

He would often just issue a **command** to individuals, such as "Go", "Get up", "Stretch out your hand". He did this to initiate an act of faith on the part of the person being healed, which in turn would activate healing. Jesus said to the centurion, "Go!"

Matthew 8:13
13 Then Jesus said to the centurion, "Go! It will
be done just as you believed it would." And his
servant was healed at that very hour.

When he healed the paralytic He said, "Get up and walk."

Luke 5:23
23 Which is easier: to say, 'Your sins are
forgiven,' or to say, 'Get up and walk'?

40

The man with the shrivelled hand was told to "Stretch out your hand," and was healed.

Luke 6:10
10 He looked around at them all, and then said to the man, "Stretch out your hand." He did so, and his hand was completely restored.

Jesus gets word from Bethany that Lazarus, the brother of Mary and Martha, is sick. I am sure that there was an expectation that He would rush to Bethany to heal Lazarus. Instead of rushing to Bethany, Jesus delayed His departure for an additional two days. By the time He got to Bethany, Lazarus had been in the tomb for four days. After they had rolled the stone away from the tomb, Jesus looked up and **prayed,** thanking His Father for hearing Him.

John 11:41-42
41 So they took away the stone. Then Jesus looked up and said, "Father, I thank you that you have heard me.
42 I knew that you always hear me, but I said this for the benefit of the people standing here, that they may believe that you sent me."

Many would come, and by just **touching** His garments, they would be totally healed. After Jesus landed at Gennesaret, the people of that area brought all their sick to Him. They begged Him to let the sick touch the edge of His cloak, and they all received healing.

Matthew 14:36
36 and begged him to let the sick just touch the edge of his cloak, and all who touched him were healed.

The woman with the issue of blood is the most widely used example of someone touching Jesus and being healed. Scripture tells us that Jesus felt the virtue, the healing power of the anointing being drawn from Him. When he had established who had touched Him, He said to her, "Daughter, your faith has healed you. Go in peace."

Luke 8:44
44 She came up behind him and touched the edge of his cloak, and immediately her bleeding stopped.

On some occasions the individual being healed would be asked to do something, to carry out an **act of faith.** The blind man was told to wash in the pool of Siloam.

John 9:7
7 "Go," he told him, "wash in the Pool of Siloam" (this word means Sent). So the man went and washed, and came home seeing.

In the case of the ten lepers, Jesus told them to go and show themselves to the priests. In both of these examples, all were completely healed.

Luke 17:14
14 When he saw them, he said, "Go, show yourselves to the priests." And as they went, they were cleansed.

There are a number of occurrences where Jesus used **spittle or mud** to heal the deaf, dumb and blind.

Mark 7:33-35
33 After he took him aside, away from the crowd, Jesus put his fingers into the man's ears. Then he spit and touched the man's tongue.
34 He looked up to heaven and with a deep sigh said to him, "Ephphatha!" (which means, "Be opened!").
35 At this, the man's ears were opened, his tongue was loosened and he began to speak plainly.

Jesus used **spittle and mud** to heal the blind man who had been blind from birth. Note that the healing was not manifested until the man washed in the pool of Siloam.

John 9:6-7
6 Having said this, he spit on the ground, made some mud with the saliva, and put it on the man's eyes.
7 "Go," he` told him, "wash in the Pool of Siloam" (this word means Sent). So the man went and washed, and came home seeing.

- **How Did He Deal With Demons?**

Jesus handled demons in a number of different ways. Sometimes He **asked the demon its name**.

Mark 5:8-9
8 For Jesus had said to him, "Come out of this man, you evil spirit!"
9 Then Jesus asked him, "What is your name?"
"My name is Legion," he replied, "for we are many."

On other occasions, he would **tell the demon(s) to be quiet.** Whether asking their name(s) or telling them to be quiet, the important thing is, that He cast them out with a **command**, as in verse 36.

Luke 4:33-36
33 In the synagogue there was a man possessed by a demon, an evil spirit. He cried out at the top of his voice,
34 "Ha! What do you want with us, Jesus of Nazareth? Have you come to destroy us? I know who you are-- the Holy One of God!"
35 "Be quiet!" Jesus said sternly. "Come out of him!" Then the demon threw the man down before them all and came out without injuring him.
36 All the people were amazed and said to each

43

other, *"What is this teaching? With authority and power he gives orders to evil spirits and they come out!"*

- **Resistance To Healing**

When Jesus encountered any resistance to healing for whatever reason, He would get quite upset. Most resistance to His ministry came from the legalist leaders of the day. When he healed the man with the withered hand, their focus was not on the healing, but on the fact that the healing had occurred on the Sabbath. The scripture says that Jesus was angry and deeply distressed at the stubbornness of their hearts.

> *Mark 3:3-5*
> *3 Jesus said to the man with the shrivelled hand, "Stand up in front of everyone."*
> *4 Then Jesus asked them, "Which is lawful on the Sabbath: to do good or to do evil, to save life or to kill?" But they remained silent.*
> *5 He looked around at them in anger and, deeply distressed at their stubborn hearts, said to the man, "Stretch out your hand." He stretched it out, and his hand was completely restored.*

When Jesus healed the woman with the spirit of infirmity on her, the ruler of the synagogue told the people to come and be healed any day but the Sabbath.

> *Luke 13:11-14*
> *11 and a woman was there who had been crippled by a spirit for eighteen years. She was bent over and could not straighten up at all.*
> *12 When Jesus saw her, he called her forward and said to her, "Woman, you are set free from your infirmity."*
> *13 Then he put his hands on her, and immediately she straightened up and praised God.*

14 Indignant because Jesus had healed on the Sabbath, the synagogue ruler said to the people, "There are six days for work. So come and be healed on those days, not on the Sabbath."

- ## The Source Of Healing

Jesus also warned His critics that his healings should not be labelled as demonic. To do so is to speak profanely of God's Holy Spirit, the result of which is removal from God's forgiveness.

Mark 3:22-29
22 And the teachers of the law who came down from Jerusalem said, "He is possessed by Beelzebub! By the prince of demons he is driving out demons
23 So Jesus called them and spoke to them in parables: "How can Satan drive out Satan?
24 If a kingdom is divided against itself, that kingdom cannot stand.
25 If a house is divided against itself, that house cannot stand.
26 And if Satan opposes himself and is divided, he cannot stand; his end has come.
27 In fact, no one can enter a strong man's house and carry off his possessions unless he first ties up the strong man. Then he can rob his house.
28 I tell you the truth, all the sins and blasphemies of men will be forgiven them.
29 But whoever blasphemes against the Holy Spirit will never be forgiven; he is guilty of an eternal sin."

Almost 20% of the text contained in the Gospels, relates to the healing ministry of Jesus. Considering that Jesus functioned continually as a healer, the percentage may seem low. The majority of the healings recorded were related to the physical and mental, not the moral conditions. I believe that it was the signs and wonders that grasped the attention of the people, and that these high profile healings were the ones that were recorded.

The Apostle John wrote that Jesus performed many other signs that were not recorded, but that those that were recorded were to help us believe. He also wrote that if all that Jesus had done had been recorded, the world would not be able to contain the books that were written. Such was the magnitude of His Healing ministry.

Overview of Jesus' Healing Ministry

Occurrence	Matt	Mark	Luke	John
Multitudes/many/crowds	4:23		6:17	
A man with leprosy	8:2	1:40	5:12	
Centurion's servant	8:5		7:2	
Peter's mother-in-law	8:14	1:30	4:38	
Multitudes/many/crowds	8:16	1:32	4:40	
Gadarenes demoniacs	8:28	5:1	8:26	
A paralytic	9:2	2:3	5:18	
Jairus' daughter	9:18	5:22	8:41	
Woman with the issue of blood	9:20	5:25	8:43	
Two blind men	9:27			
Dumb demoniac	9:32			
Multitudes/many/crowds	9:35			
Man with a shriveled hand	12:10	3:1	6:6	
Multitudes/many/crowds	12:15	3:10		
Blind and mute demoniac	12:22		11:14	
Few/not many	13:58	6:5		
Multitudes/many/crowds	14:14		9:11	6:2
Multitudes/many/crowds	14:35	6:55		
Syrophoenician's daughter	15:22	7:24		
Multitudes/many/crowds	15:30			

Occurrence	Matt	Mark	Luke	John
Boy with a demon	17:14	9:14	9:38	
Multitudes/many/crowds	19:2			
Blind Bartimeus	20:30	10:46	18:35	
Blind and lame in temple	21:14			
Man possessed by a demon		1:23	4:33	
Deaf and mute man		7:32		
Blind man at Bethsaida		8:22		
Multitudes/many/crowds			5:15	
Widow's son			7:11	
Multitudes/many/crowds			7:21	
Mary Magdalene and others			8:2	
Woman bound by Satan			13:10	
Various persons			13:32	
Man with dropsy			14:1	
Ten lepers			17:11	
Malcus' ear			22:50	
The officials son				4:46
Invalid at the pool of Bethesda				5:2
Man born blind				9:1
Lazarus				11:1

Chapter 5

Healing In The New Testament

Jesus came to remove us from under the power and influence of Satan, and to set us free from the oppression of the principalities of darkness. He stated this when He read from the scroll of the prophet Isaiah, in the synagogue in Nazareth. What He read was Isaiah's foretelling of His ministry of preaching and healing that would meet every human need.

> **Luke 4:18**
> **18 "The Spirit of the Lord is on me, because he has anointed me to preach good news to the poor. He has sent me to proclaim freedom for the prisoners and recovery of sight for the blind, to release the oppressed,**

The healing that Jesus brought, covers every aspect of healing that is required to provide wholeness for the believer. It not only encompasses the physical, mental, and spiritual, but also includes the environment surrounding us.

- **From Death To Life**

The greatest act of faith that a believer is required to perform is the believing for, and receiving of, salvation. Salvation in itself is healing, the restoration of a relationship between an individual and God. In the scriptures, the word used for healing is often the same word that is translated as salvation, and both healing and salvation are used when referring to wholeness in the life of a believer. The healing that Jesus brought enables us as believers to make the transition from death to life.

> *John 5:24*
> *24 "I tell you the truth, whoever hears my word and believes him who sent me has eternal life and will not be condemned; he has crossed over from death to life.*

It is the Greek word, *sozo*, which is used for both healing and salvation. The word literally means, "saved out from under the devil's power and restored into the wholeness of God's order by the power of the Holy Spirit." The scriptures tell us that when Christ redeems us, we are a new creation, made brand new, made totally whole, and what we used to be is gone.

> *2 Corinthians 5:17*
> *17 Therefore, if anyone is in Christ, he is a new creation; the old has gone, the new has 'come!*

The healing that is brought about by redemption, is the complete and total restoration of God's purpose and plan for our lives.

- **Forgiveness Of Sin**

It is the shed blood of Jesus that initiates the new blood covenant. This new covenant in His blood, was initiated to provide man with forgiveness of sin, and to bring man back into relationship with God.

Matthew 26:28
28 This is my blood of the covenant, which is poured out for many for the forgiveness of sins.

Jesus took the sin of man upon Himself, that we might become the righteousness of God.

2 Corinthians 5:21
21 God made him who had no sin to be sin for us, so that in him we might become the righteousness of God.

This gift of forgiveness that God has given us, releases healing to every aspect of our lives that are affected by sin. Having given us His forgiveness, God then desires that we remain free of guilt, condemnation, unworthiness or any other lie that Satan himself might want us to believe.

Romans 8:1
1 Therefore, there is now no condemnation for those who are in Christ Jesus,

It is so important that every believer understands this, the very one who sacrificed His life for us, is that same one who now sits at the right hand of the Father, making intercession for us. If Jesus held any anything against us, He would not be able to petition on our behalf.

Rom 8:31-34
31 What, then, shall we say in response to this? If God is for us, who can be against us?
32 He who did not spare his own Son, but gave him up for us all—how will he not also, along with him, graciously give us all things?
33 Who will bring any charge against those whom God has chosen? It is God who justifies.
34 Who is he that condemns? Christ Jesus, who died-- more than that, who was raised to life-- is

at the right hand of God and is also interceding for us.

By actively and continually believing in God's forgiveness, we will overcome the "accuser of the brethren." We are saved, healed, restored, made whole, forgiven, made righteous, and able to hold our heads up high, in the full knowledge that Jesus is with the Father telling Him all about us.

- **Restoration From Sickness and Disease**

The prophet Isaiah wrote that we are to be strong and not fear, for God comes with a vengeance and divine retribution to save us. God is so anxious and concerned about our physical and spiritual well being, that He can hardly wait to heal us, or the situation we are in. He will come to support our cause, and will dispense justice and punishment to those who would come against us.

> *Isaiah 35:3-6*
> *3 Strengthen the feeble hands, steady the knees that give way;*
> *4 say to those with fearful hearts, "Be strong, do not fear; your God will come, he will come with vengeance; with divine retribution he will come to save you."*
> *5 Then will the eyes of the blind be opened and the ears of the deaf unstopped.*
> *6 Then will the lame leap like a deer, and the mute tongue shout for joy. Water will gush forth in the wilderness and streams in the desert.*

With the coming of Jesus, everything in this scripture from Isaiah was fulfilled. Jesus was filled with the same compassion, the same desires, and the same motives as His Father. He not only came to restore people from sickness and disease, He came to destroy the source of it. He came to destroy the works of Satan. When John the Baptist sent his followers to ask if He was the one who was to come, Jesus responded by telling them to go and report what they had heard and seen.

Matthew 11:3-5
3 to ask him, "Are you the one who was to come,
or should we expect someone else?"
4 Jesus replied, "Go back and report to John what
you hear and see:
5 The blind receive sight, the lame walk, those
who have leprosy are cured, the deaf hear, the
dead are raised, and the good news is preached
to the poor.

The power and anointing of the Holy Spirit was on Him, and He healed all who were under the power of Satan.

Acts 10:38
38 how God anointed Jesus of Nazareth with the
Holy Spirit and power, and how he went around
doing good and healing all who were under the
power of the devil, because God was with him.

Jesus healed every kind of sickness and disease. He healed in the physical, mental and spiritual. He fulfilled the scripture spoken through the prophet Isaiah, when He took on all of our infirmities and diseases.

Matthew 8:16-17
16 When evening came, many who were demon-
possessed were brought to him, and he drove out
the spirits with a word and healed all the sick.
17 This was to fulfill what was spoken through
the prophet Isaiah: "He took up our infirmities
and carried our diseases."

Jesus came to destroy the works of the devil. Every aspect of Satan's agenda will be destroyed. Satan's policy of sickness, disease and death is finished, because of what Jesus did at Calvary.

1 John 3:8
8 He who does what is sinful is of the devil,
because the devil has been sinning from the

beginning. The reason the Son of God appeared was to destroy the devil's work.

Satan's works are destroyed one person at a time, and this is why it is so important that we as believers witness at every opportunity. If we see sickness and disease, we should be laying on hands and praying for healing. We, as believers, are empowered by the Holy Spirit, and we are responsible for doing God's work on earth until He returns.

- **Deliverance From Demonic Power**

In the New Testament church, the most dramatic healings were those involving the deliverance from demonic power. When Jesus cast out demons, they knew who He was, and they knew His position of authority being "the Holy One of God." The fact that they left at His command is confirmation that they recognized His authority.

> *Mark 1:24*
> *24 "What do you want with us, Jesus of Nazareth? Have you come to destroy us? I know who you are-- the Holy One of God!"*

The authority and power that Jesus walked in, has been passed onto those who believe. Many believers, some of which are pastors, tend to shy away from this area of healing. I have heard it described as a front line ministry, almost as if you are required to participate in hand to hand combat with demonic forces, in order for them to leave. It is not this way at all! It is part of the healing ministry that we as believers are to carry on until the Lord returns. I would encourage those who are apprehensive of this area of healing, to consider this point, **"It is not you who is doing the work, it's God."**

Jesus placed much emphasis on maintaining the healing (deliverance) where a demonic force or presence has been dealt with. The scripture in Matthew 12:43-45 details exactly what can happen if the demonic force or presence is allowed to return. The key word here is **"allowed"**. The enemy is only allowed in if we open a door. Once the enemy is removed and the door is closed, he cannot enter back in unless the door is opened again. If a particular sin was the initial cause of the demonic force or presence, and if after the removal the individual falls back into that same sin, the outcome is seven times worse than before.

> *Matthew 12:43-45*
> *43 "When an evil spirit comes out of a man, it goes through arid places seeking rest and does not find it.*
> *44 Then it says, 'I will return to the house I left.' When it arrives, it finds the house unoccupied, swept clean and put in order.*
> *45 Then it goes and takes with it seven other spirits more wicked than itself, and they go in and live there. And the final condition of that man is worse than the first. That is how it will be with this wicked generation."*

Some time ago, my ministry team and I were called in to minister to an individual, whom I shall refer to as John. We dealt with a number of demons that John was carrying within, and all were expelled. We then concentrated our efforts on cleaning out his home, which was also carried out successfully. Over the next few months, we were called in to repeat the process two more times. After each ministry session, John was warned that if he continued to open doors that the situation would just get worse. Regrettably, he chose to re-open the doors, allowing demonic forces to enter back in and wreak havoc with his mental capacity, resulting in John taking his own life.

- **More Abundant Life**

The hunger, the poverty, the droughts, the floods, the famine, and the general lack that we see in the world today, are all part of the curse that was spoken over Adam after the fall. Jesus has removed you and I from under the curse of the law by becoming a curse for us.

Galatians 3:13
13 Christ redeemed us from the curse of the law
by becoming a curse for us, for it is written:
"Cursed is everyone who is hung on a tree."

Jesus, being the Son of God, undoubtedly had infinite riches. Through His incarnation and His subsequent death on the cross, Jesus emptied Himself of all His riches. What more could Jesus give? Paul writes in Philippians 2:7-9, that Jesus humbled Himself, becoming obedient to death, and God exalted Him to the highest place. Jesus gave all that he had for you and I, and in return, His Father elevated Him to the highest. My study Bible notes that this is the supreme incentive of all Christian generosity. Jesus gave it all for you and I.

2 Corinthians 8:9
9 For you know the grace of our Lord Jesus
Christ, that though he was rich, yet for your sakes
he became poor, so that you through his poverty
might become rich.

The early Christian church was a prosperous church. There was no poverty mentality because the believers were free in sharing God's abundance with their brothers and sisters. There was a unity in the hearts and minds of the believers, that birthed a genuine desire to see that everyone had all of their needs met. This was not focussed on purely financial or material needs, but on every need. In the book of Acts we are told, "there was no needy persons among them."

Acts 4:32-35
32 All the believers were one in heart and mind.
No one claimed that any of his possessions was
his own, but they shared everything they had.
33 With great power the apostles continued to
testify to the resurrection of the Lord Jesus, and
much grace was upon them all.
34 There were no needy persons among them.
For from time to time those who owned lands or
houses sold them, brought the money from the

sales
35 and put it at the apostles' feet, and it was distributed to anyone as he had need.

As believers, we are to be successful in everything that we do, and we are to walk in abundance. By being successful and walking in abundance, we are then able to give to those in need. As God releases His blessings to us, we must be prepared to bless others, in doing so, we will bring glory to His name.

2 Corinthians 9:9-11
9 As it is written: "He has scattered abroad his gifts to the poor; his righteousness endures forever."
10 Now he who supplies seed to the sower and bread for food will also supply and increase your store of seed and will enlarge the harvest of your righteousness.
11 You will be made rich in every way so that you can be generous on every occasion, and through us your generosity will result in thanksgiving to God.

The more abundant life is the only way to go. I don't know anyone who has ever enjoyed being in poverty. I can only tell you that from my own personal experience, when I give from my abundance, God always gives me back more than I have given.

Overview of the Healing Ministry of Others in the New Testament

Occurrence	Matt	Mark	Luke	Acts
Jesus sends out the twelve	10:1	3:14	9:1	
The power to bind and loose	16:19			
Disciples fail to cast out demon	17:16	9:17	9:40	
The Great Commission	28:18	16:15		
Whoever is not against us, is for us		9:38		
Jesus sends out the seventy-two			10:1	
Signs and wonders at the hands of the Apostles				2:43
Peter heals a crippled beggar				3:6
Signs and wonders at the hands of the Apostles				5:12
The Ministry of Stephen				6:8
The Ministry of Phillip				8:6
Saul's sight is restored				9:10
Peter heals Aeneas in Lydda				9:32
Peter raises Tabitha (Dorcas) from the dead				9:39
Paul and Barnabas at Iconium				14:3
Paul heals lame man in Lystra				14:8

Occurrence	Matt	Mark	Luke	Acts
Paul raised up at Lystra				14:19
The slave girl at Philippi				16:16
Paul in Ephesus				19:11
Eutychus raised from the dead in Troas				20:9
Paul on Malta				28:3

Chapter 6

Wrong Teaching

Since becoming a believer, I have attended and been involved in a number of churches of various denominations. It would be fair to say that only one of the churches I have attended saw regular manifestations of divine healing. Due to a lack of manifestation of divine healing, many pastors and teachers have relegated this Doctrine of Christ to the back burner. Instead of bringing their congregations up to greater level of understanding, they have diluted the word of God to a level that is acceptable to their congregations. Without proper teaching, without proper understanding of God's Word, the people of God will never be able to address the issues, that are preventing the healing anointing of the Holy Spirit from moving in their churches.

Beware all you pastors and teachers out there, particularly those who are not teaching their flocks what the word says about divine health and divine healing. In Hosea's time, the priests were punished because they were guilty of not giving proper instruction to the people. The scripture in Hosea 4:6 is frequently quoted when referring to people not knowing, "my people are destroyed from lack of knowledge." It is the latter part of the verse where the meat is, "Because you have rejected knowledge, I also reject you as my priests." While it is certainly about people not knowing, it's more about people not being taught.

> **Hosea 4:6-9**
> *6 my people are destroyed from lack of knowledge. "Because you have rejected knowledge, I also reject you as my priests; because you have ignored the law of your God, I also will ignore your children.*
> *7 The more the priests increased, the more they sinned against me; they exchanged their Glory for something disgraceful.*
> *8 They feed on the sins of my people and relish their wickedness.*
> *9 And it will be: Like people, like priests. I will punish both of them for their ways and repay them for their deeds.*

Many believers in today's church are walking in sickness and disease that will result in physical death. They are in this condition because they have not been taught who they are and what they have access to. Some have been taught that healing was only for Jesus' time and not for the church of this era. The result is that most of these people will never walk in divine health or experience divine healing. Some denominations have succeeded in putting God in a box, and they only let Him out to do the things that their particular denomination believes in. The outcome of this is that the moving of the Holy Spirit is severely limited, and in many cases it is totally quenched, all because of man-made doctrine.

One thing can be said about the New Testament church, it was based on sound doctrine. The term Apostle's Doctrine was used to describe the material taught by the apostles, all of which was consistent with scripture. The New Testament church formed after Pentecost was responsible for recording and maintaining the purity of the material taught by the apostles. As the number of churches grew, they came under the authority of God by adhering to the recorded material and scripture. Today, through the Bible and many other documents, the church has access to all of this material.

The example set by leadership certainly goes hand-in-hand with wrong teaching. The relationship between a pastor or teacher and their flock, can be compared to the relationship between a parent and sibling. A sibling will listen to what the parent says, but will most likely do what the parent does. If those in leadership are not walking in divine health or have not been able to access divine healing, what message does that send to their congregation? It is extremely difficult for a pastor or teacher to preach or teach on the subject of divine health or divine healing, if they are not manifesting one or the other.

As I mentioned earlier, in one of the churches I attended, there was a great outpouring of God's healing anointing. After a great time of healings and peoples lives being turned around, it dwindled and died. It is important that I explain to you what happened so that you don't have the same thing happen to your church. Initially, there was a strong core group of believers who were in unity, and who were praying and believing for healings to take place. The leadership at that time were walking in a level of obedience and humility that was acceptable to God. God moved in accordance with His Word and His will, and the healing anointing flowed. People came from all over and many were healed from all manners of sickness and disease.

In a very short period of time a number of critical things happened. The leadership allowed pride to creep in, and this caused the core group to be reduced in size, which caused the effective prayer to be diminished. Along with the pride came a little gossip, a little unforgiveness, a little of this and a little of that, and so on. It was so subtle, it happened a little at a time, until the manifestation of the healing anointing was a thing of the past. When the leadership of a vibrant ministry removes itself from the will of God, that ministry is doomed to die. The scripture in James 3:1 emphasises that those who teach (leadership) will be judged more strictly.

James 3:1
1 Not many of you should presume to be teachers, my brothers, because you know that we who teach will be judged more strictly.

In this day and age, there is absolutely no excuse for any pastor or teacher, not to teach what is written in God's Word. A pastor friend of mine says it all when he states, "Teach what you know, impart what you are". If you are in leadership and you teach your people well, you will empower them to walk in divine health, and if required, enable them to activate divine healing. Having taught them well it is just as important that you live and walk in what you have taught.

Chapter 7

Authority And Power

The word authority **(Gk. *exousia*)** means the freedom and right to exercise the power that God has given to us. The word power **(Gk. *dunamis*)** means the miraculous power to work miracles. As believers, **we have the freedom and right to exercise God's miraculous power to work miracles.** If we fully understand our rights, and choose to exercise God's authority to heal, we will be just like Jesus to those in need. While God still maintains absolute authority, He has delegated this authority and power to every believer so that we might fulfil the commission that we have been given.

In this world, authority and power are usually associated with a position within an organization or structure. In the spiritual realm, power and authority are viewed from a relational aspect, and will only be released to those with a servant's heart. Authority and power will be released to those who will use it to minister help to their fellow man, and in doing so bring glory to God.

Matthew 20:25-26
25 Jesus called them together and said, "You know that the rulers of the Gentiles lord it over them, and their high officials exercise authority over them.

26 Not so with you. Instead, whoever wants to
become great among you must be your servant,

God, having created man for His pleasure, for His glory, and
to fulfil His plan and His purpose, means that man has a special
relationship with Him. The scope of this relationship provides man
with a unique identity and a position of authority within creation
itself. God made man in His image and gave him the authority to rule
over all the earth and everything in it.

Genesis 1:26
26 Then God said, "Let us make man in our
image, in our likeness, and let them rule over the
fish of the sea and the birds of the air, over the
livestock, over all the earth, and over all the
creatures that move along the ground."

The Psalmist David writes in Psalm 8:6, that God made us
ruler over all the works of His hands, and put everything under our
feet.

Psalm 8:6
6 You made him ruler over the works of your
hands; you put everything under his feet:

As a result of the sin of Adam and Eve, man was not only
driven from the garden, but was also removed from his position of
authority. Satan's deception and the resulting sin of rebellion against
God's command enabled Satan to remove man from power. Satan
then became Prince, Ruler and God of this world. The Apostle Paul
when writing to the church at Corinth, acknowledges Satan as the
god of this age.

2 Corinthians 4:4
4 The god of this age has blinded the minds of
unbelievers, so that they cannot see the light of
the gospel of the glory of Christ, who is the image
of God.

All of creation became enslaved under the authority and jurisdiction of Satan. His total policy of sin, sickness and disease, oppression and depression, became a reality for mankind. As long as Satan was in control, those in sin could not break out from under it on their own power. Not until Cavalry's cross, was man provided with an avenue of escape through Salvation.

John 8:34
34 Jesus replied, "I tell you the truth, everyone who sins is a slave to sin.

After being baptized in the Jordan River, Jesus was led by the Spirit into the desert. For forty days, Jesus was tempted by the devil. During this time, the devil led Him to a high place and showed Him all the kingdoms of the world. The devil offered Jesus all their authority and splendour in exchange for Jesus worshipping him. The scripture in Luke 4:6, tells us that it was the devil's authority and splendour to give, because it had been given to him and he could do what he wanted with it.

Luke 4:6
6 And he said to him, "I will give you all their authority and splendor, for it has been given to me, and I can give it to anyone I want to.

The reason that God sent Jesus as a man, and not as Himself, was so that Satan could not cry, "Foul." God sent His only begotten Son to earth as a man, as the second Adam, to re-establish God's authority over the earth. Jesus was sent to disarm all satanic powers and so remove man out from under their authority. After being tempted by the devil, Jesus returned to Galilee, eventually arriving at His hometown of Nazareth. On the Sabbath day Jesus went to the synagogue where He read from the scroll of the prophet Isaiah. What he read publicly established the scope of His ministry.

Luke 4:14-18
14 Jesus returned to Galilee in the power of the Spirit, and news about him spread through the whole countryside.

15 He taught in their synagogues, and everyone praised him.

16 He went to Nazareth, where he had been brought up, and on the Sabbath day he went into the synagogue, as was his custom. And he stood up to read.

17 The scroll of the prophet Isaiah was handed to him. Unrolling it, he found the place where it is written:

18 "The Spirit of the Lord is on me, because he has anointed me to preach good news to the poor. He has sent me to proclaim freedom for the prisoners and recovery of sight for the blind, to release the oppressed,

As in integral part of the Trinity, Jesus had an intimate relationship with the Father. He knew who he was, and what He had access to. Jesus knew the authority that He walked in, and that His authority came from his relationship with the Father. Jesus knew what He had been called to do and was obedient to the Father even unto death.

John 17:2
2 For you granted him authority over all people that he might give eternal life to all those you have given him.

Knowing the Fathers love, and that the Father had placed everything in His hands, helps explain His boldness as He exercised the authority given to Him.

John 3:35
35 The Father loves the Son and has placed everything in his hands.

As stated previously, through His life, death and resurrection, Jesus disarmed and defeated the spiritual powers of the prince of this world.

John 12:31
31 Now is the time for judgment on this world;
now the prince of this world will be driven out.

Having bled and died at Calvary, Jesus removed Satan from power. Man through His shed blood is once again able to come into relationship with God, once again having become the righteousness of God.

2 Corinthians 5:21
21 God made him who had no sin to be sin for us,
so that in him we might become the righteousness of God.

Man's new relationship with God is not like the one that Adam once had. Adam had been able to walk and talk and have fellowship with God in the garden. In our new relationship, God has made us alive in Christ, through grace our sins have been forgiven. Now that Jesus is seated at the right hand of the Father, God has raised us up and we are seated with Him.

Ephesians 2:4-6
4 But because of his great love for us, God, who is rich in mercy,
5 made us alive with Christ even when we were dead in transgressions--it is by grace you have been saved.
6 And God raised us up with Christ and seated us with him in the heavenly realms in Christ Jesus,

We believers, who are part of the body of Christ, have been given a commission. Since Jesus has been given all authority in heaven and on earth, we are to go in His authority, and in His name. We are to:-

- Heal the sick
- Raise the dead
- Drive out demons

Matthew 10:8
8 Heal the sick, raise the dead, cleanse those who have leprosy, drive out demons. Freely you have received, freely give.

Before going to be with the Father, Jesus appeared to his disciple for the last time. He delivered what has come to be known as The Great Commission. This commission has been handed down to you and I and we are to:-

- Make disciples of all nations
- Baptize them
- Teach them to obey

Matthew 28:18-20
18 Then Jesus came to them and said, "All authority in heaven and on earth has been given to me.
19 Therefore go and make disciples of all nations, baptizing them in the name of the Father and of the Son and of the Holy Spirit,
20 and teaching them to obey everything I have commanded you. And surely I am with you always, to the very end of the age."

Jesus has given us authority over the all the power of the enemy, without fear of harm.

Luke 10:19
19 I have given you authority to trample on snakes and scorpions and to overcome all the power of the enemy; nothing will harm you.

He has also provided for us the comforter who is the Holy Spirit, which came down at Pentecost.

Acts 1:8
8 But you will receive power when the Holy Spirit comes on you; and you will be my witnesses in

Jerusalem, and in all Judea and Samaria, and to the ends of the earth. "

The authority to heal has to be exercised. If we do not believe what God says, our lack of faith will negate our authority. We need to know and believe our position in the body, and know the commission we have been given. We need to know and believe what God has done through Jesus Christ in terms of destroying the enemy and his works. Faith in God brings a release of authority, and authority is released through service as you minister. The more you do it, the greater your authority will become. Speak the word, speak to the sickness or disease and command it to be gone "In Jesus' name."

Chapter 8

Why Do Believers Fall Sick?

The primary cause of sickness in the body of Christ is personal Sin. What is Sin? Sin is the breaking of a divine or moral law, especially by a conscious act. Because God is a Holy God, and cannot be in the presence of sin, when we commit a sin our communion with Him is broken. Then, just like Adam and Eve in the garden; we are removed from God's divine protection. That protection can take the form of divine health or divine healing. Our divine protection, our covering is removed, doors are opened, and we are then exposed to the powers and principalities of darkness. We then come under the jurisdiction of Satan, and become subject to his policy of sickness and disease. Don't forget that Satan comes to steal, kill and destroy

Ephesians 6:12
12 For our struggle is not against flesh and blood, but against the rulers, against the authorities, against the powers of this dark world and against the spiritual forces of evil in the heavenly realms.

If we sin intentionally or otherwise, we should not be surprised if we end up with some form of sickness or disease. Having broken a spiritual law, we are subject to the penalty. When talking about sin, I often use the analogy of being pregnant, my apologies to the ladies. You are either pregnant or you are not, you cannot be half pregnant. Sin falls in the same category, you are either in sin or you are not, you can't half sin. We are so fortunate that through grace, God allows us to repent, request and receive His divine healing, no matter what the situation is. The scriptures tell us that all have sinned.

> ***Romans 3:23***
> ***23 for all have sinned and fall short of the glory of God,***

God in His infinite mercy has provided us with an avenue of escape through His son Jesus.

> ***John 1:29***
> ***29 The next day John saw Jesus coming toward him and said, "Look, the Lamb of God, who takes away the sin of the world!***

In addition to personal sin, we must also consider the effects of generational sin. God told the people of Israel that the sins of the father would carry on for four generations. Many believe that this curse was only for Old Testament times. Let me assure you that it's just as relevant today as it was back then.

> ***Exodus 20:5***
> ***5 You shall not bow down to them or worship them; for I, the LORD your God, am a jealous God, punishing the children for the sin of the fathers to the third and fourth generation of those who hate me,***

Many causes of sickness and disease are directly related to the sins of our fathers. For example: in my family, both my grandfather and my father died of heart disease. I will not die of heart disease, because I have broken the generational curse that was hanging over my family. I simply broke the power of the curse and released divine healing to heal any damage done. I would certainly recommend to all readers, that you look for any trends or patterns of sickness and

74

disease that have affected your family. If you find any, and you probably will, break the power of the curse and release healing for any damage done.

Some time back, a pastor friend of mine fell ill and was bedridden. I made arrangements to go over and visit with him. When I arrived and saw how ill he was, and my immediate thought was that he was going home to be with the Lord. We wept together as I prayed for him. When I left his home, I left extremely distressed over his condition, and not sure if I would see him again on this earth. Thankfully, God still answers prayers, and my friend was restored back to health, and was able to hear me speak on the subject of Divine Healing. I used him as an example of what happens when you break **the physical laws**.

My friend was not a young man any more, now in his seventies, he was still trying to do it all. He was overworked, cleaning the church, counselling, taking phone calls, preparing teachings and preaching, all with little or no help. He was right with God, he was not wilfully disobedient to God, he just expected too much from an aging body.

Too many believers are in this situation today. Take a look at the church in North America, most of us are overweight, one in three are obese. Two out of three of our school-aged children are overweight. If we fail to properly care for our bodies, and sickness and disease are the result, that's not God's will. If we overeat and don't exercise, we can end up with high blood pressure and high cholesterol. This is why many of us are prime candidates for heart attacks or strokes. There are many believers who still smoke cigarettes, still consume alcohol, still do a little drugs, and justify it on the basis that God hasn't removed the desire from them yet. Our bodies are the temple of the Holy Spirit, should we not be keeping God's house clean?

1 Corinthians 3:16
16 Don't you know that you yourselves are God's temple and that God's Spirit lives in you?

Not only are our bodies the temple of the Holy Spirit, we have also given up ownership of our bodies. They are not our own, there are His. If they belong to God, why would God want us to bring sickness, disease, or physical death on His temple? God wants to see us bring Him glory; and there is no glory in sickness, disease or physical death.

> **1 Corinthians 6:19**
> **19 Do you not know that your body is a temple of the Holy Spirit, who is in you, whom you have received from God? You are not your own;**

There is also a warning to us, that God's temple is sacred and it is important to Him. We are to maintain both our spiritual and physical health because we were created for His glory.

> **1 Corinthians 3:17**
> **17 If anyone destroys God's temple, God will destroy him; for God's temple is sacred, and you are that temple.**

As believers, we need to recognize that God is not glorified if we walk in sickness or disease. We have been promised divine health, and when we require it, we have access to divine healing. As believers, our primary focus should be on maintaining the former and not becoming dependant on the latter. Many believers today, accept as normal, the occasional or even regular occurrence of sickness followed by healing. Because so many have accepted this as being normal, it has been accepted as God's plan for us. This is not what God's word says, His word says that it is not divine healing but divine health that is His plan for us.

Chapter 9

Why Do Some Not Receive Healing?

Divine healing falls into the same category as divine health; the effectiveness of either is directly related to the spiritual condition of the individual. Just as Sin is the primary cause of sickness, it is also the primary cause of some individuals not being healed. In the New Testament, Jesus often said to the person being healed that his or her sins were forgiven instead of saying that he or she was healed.

> *Matthew 9:2-6*
> *2 Some men brought to him a paralytic, lying on a mat. When Jesus saw their faith, he said to the paralytic, "Take heart, son; your sins are forgiven."*
> *3 At this, some of the teachers of the law said to themselves, "This fellow is blaspheming!"*
> *4 Knowing their thoughts, Jesus said, "Why do you entertain evil thoughts in your hearts?*
> *5 Which is easier: to say, `Your sins are forgiven,' or to say, `Get up and walk'?*
> *6 But so that you may know that the Son of Man has authority on earth to forgive sins...." Then he said to the paralytic, "Get up, take your mat and go home."*

If sin causes sickness and disease, then surely sin can prevent the manifestation of the healing. As I have previously mentioned, sin breaks our communion with God and does not permit Him to allow us access to His divine healing. It is important to remember that the greatest example of healing is when we receive Salvation, and we cannot receive Salvation without repentance of sin.

We know the story of how Jesus healed the man at the pool of Bethesda. In John 5:14, we are told that later, Jesus found him in the temple and told him to stop sinning or something worse would happen to him. The implication here is that if he continued to sin, that he would lose his healing and a greater calamity would befall him. This is a serious warning! This man had been an invalid for thirty-eight years, and if he did not stop sinning, something worse was going to happen to him.

> *John 5:14*
> *14 Later Jesus found him at the temple and said to him, "See, you are well again. Stop sinning or something worse may happen to you."*

In this same chapter there are two more very important points. Firstly, Jesus tells the Jews that His Father is always working and that He is working also.

> *John 5:17*
> *17 Jesus said to them, "My Father is always at his work to this very day, and I, too, am working."*

Secondly, He tells them that He does nothing that He does not see the Father doing. In other words, Jesus healed no one on His own initiative; He was obedient to the revelation He received from His father. What Jesus did through His ministry, was to confirm to the world, that it is God's will that all would be healed.

> *John 5:19*
> *19 Jesus gave them this answer: "I tell you the truth, the Son can do nothing by himself; he can do only what he sees his Father doing, because whatever the Father does the Son also does.*

These same basic truths still hold true for today. God desires that we would walk in divine health. Where there is sickness and disease, He desires to see us healed. Sin, in any one of it's many forms, can and will prevent, the healing anointing from flowing and manifesting a much needed healing.

After Sin, the next major hindrance to receiving healing is the lack of knowledge of God's word. Just as in the Old Testament, it is the obligation of God's people to know His word. Jesus, in Matthew 5, states that He did not come to abolish the Law or the Prophets, but that He was the fulfillment of them.

Matthew 5:17
17 "Do not think that I have come to abolish the Law or the Prophets; I have not come to abolish them but to fulfill them.

This being the case, God's instructions to the people of Israel back in Exodus 15:26 still apply to the church of this age. Just as the Ten Commandments still apply, God's covenant of healing still applies. If we are to avoid the diseases that God brought on the Egyptians and maintain divine health, we are instructed to do the following:

1. **Listen carefully to the voice of the Lord your God.**
2. **Do what is right in His eyes.**
3. **Pay attention to all His commands.**
4. **Keep all His decrees.**

If we do not know what God's word says about divine health and divine healing, how can we know our birthright? Some in the church actually believe that sickness is inevitable, and that occasional sickness is to be expected. My bible says that I am to walk in divine health, and if sickness does come upon me, that I have access to divine healing. Nowhere in my bible does it say that sickness, occasional or otherwise, is God's plan for my life. If I am walking in sickness, how can I be representative of the glory of God?

This whole concept of there being glory in sickness is founded on the story of Jesus healing the blind man. For some, this scripture has become their own Doctrine of Sickness and Disease.

> *John 9:1-3*
> *1 As he went along, he saw a man blind from birth.*
> *2 His disciples asked him, "Rabbi, who sinned, this man or his parents, that he was born blind?"*
> *3 "Neither this man nor his parents sinned," said Jesus, "but this happened so that the work of God might be displayed in his life.*

I have heard this very scripture being used to justify the presence of cancer in the life of a believer. The individual in question told me that God had allowed her to contract cancer so that she could minister to others. When she died a few months later, I couldn't help wondering how God was glorified in her death. She left behind a family that gradually drifted away from the church, because they felt that God had let them down. If only she had put as much effort into claiming, receiving, and declaring her healing, then God would certainly have been glorified in her recovery.

This event detailed in John 9:1-3 is the only one that states that God caused an individual to have an infirmity. God is God! If God chose to cause this particular individual to have an infirmity, who are we to dispute this? We cant, but what we can do, is to declare the word that states we are to walk in divine health, and if necessary claim divine healing. If you are walking in sickness and disease, don't waste your time blaming God for you circumstances, get right with God and claim your healing.

No material on healing would be complete without a reference to faith, or the lack thereof. The Apostle Paul states what faith is in Hebrews 11:1

> *Hebrews 11:1*
> *1 Now faith is being sure of what we hope for and certain of what we do not see.*

80

In Romans 10:17, the Apostle Paul tells us how we acquire faith. He tells us that faith is acquired through hearing the message, which is heard through the word of Christ.

Romans 10:17
17 Consequently, faith comes from hearing the message, and the message is heard through the word of Christ.

If we do not know God's word or message, if we do not read it, if we do not hear it, we can never come into the knowledge of what is contained in it. Faith is always based on something; you can't have faith based on nothing. The faith to believe for healing can only be based on God's word.

2 Corinthians 5:7
7 We live by faith, not by sight.

Satan has really done a number on the church of Jesus Christ. He has blinded so many to their birthright. Many walk in sickness and disease, and many have died or are dying because they do not know who they are in Christ. Knowledge of God's word will enable you to enjoy a victorious walk that will bring Him glory.

As individuals, God has graciously allowed us to have much personal choice with regards to our relationship with Him. This holds true even when we are in need of healing. It never ceases to amaze me how some believers can choose to believe for the healing of others, but cannot believe for themselves. The reason I state that it is a choice, is because I know that God is no respecter of persons. He views us all equally; and if we are all of equal worth and value in His sight, we all have equal access to healing. God has no favourites.

Acts 10:34
34 Then Peter began to speak: "I now realize how true it is that God does not show favoritism

Satan on the other hand is the father of lies. He has convinced many that they are too unworthy to receive healing, too insignificant in the eyes of God. Have you ever asked yourself the question, "Why would God heal me?" Have you thought to yourself, "I'm not deserving." These two lies along with many others, have held many believers in the bondage of sickness.

> *John 8:44*
> *44 You belong to your father, the devil, and you want to carry out your father's desire. He was a murderer from the beginning, not holding to the truth, for there is no truth in him. When he lies, he speaks his native language, for he is a liar and the father of lies.*

Many believers have chosen to wallow in self-pity, moaning and complaining about their symptoms. Out of one side of their mouth they will tell you that they are healed, while out of the other you get the latest medical gobbledygook about their condition. They will tell you that while in the natural they experience all these symptoms, that in the spiritual realm they are totally healed. Instead of being victorious, these people allow themselves to become the victims of their feelings, emotions and symptoms. They literally create for themselves a form of bondage. They are so busy dealing with the symptoms that they fail to deal with the sickness.

> *Proverbs 16:25*
> *25 There is a way that seems right to a man, but in the end it leads to death.*

Some believers have made a friend of their sickness. When Jesus approached the lame man at the pool of Bethesda, He asked the man if he wanted to be healed. In that time, the beggars, the lame and infirm could all make a good living from their sickness

> *John 5:6*
> *6 When Jesus saw him lying there and learned that he had been in this condition for a long time, he asked him, "Do you want to get well?"*

82

Many believers have chosen a particular lifestyle, which exposes them to things that are not of God. The result of this is that many are failing to obey one or more scriptural requirement. Since they are not in line with God's word, healing is not always forthcoming.

Chapter 10

Why Do Some Lose Their Healing?

Whether reading in the Old Testament or in the New, it is quite obvious that divine healing is generally sought as a last resort. As I have already stated in the introduction, I can certainly speak from experience in this area. In the course of my sickness, I had exhausted the medical technology of the time, and I had no one else to turn to. So, in desperation, as a last resort, I turned to God. When I went forward for prayer at the Saturday night meeting, I had only been saved a couple of weeks. I have since learned that there is no better time to receive from God, than when you have first received Him as Lord and Saviour. My faith was at it's strongest, and my mind had not become cluttered with man-made doctrine. And most important of all, no one had told me that I could not be healed!

Over the years I have attended a number of Crusades or Healing services, and I have seen the hand of God move mightily. At these Crusades or Healing services, I have discovered that there are a number of common denominators.

1. **The participants go with expectation - they expect to be healed.**
2. **There is an air of repentance - barriers are down.**

3. There is air of corporate faith - common unity and purpose.
4. No outside interference - God focused.
5. No negativity - no one to tell them that they will not receive healing.

I was watching a TV ministry one day where a group were discussing the ministry of the late Katherine Kuhlman. This great woman of God saw countless thousands healed at her meetings, yet many lost their healing shortly thereafter. The sceptics in the group were having a field day; they had downgraded genuine healings to emotional experiences. Regrettably, it is true that many receive healing and lose it after a time. Why is this so? Some of the major reasons are:-

As stated previously, repentance is a common theme at these meetings. It is quite normal to hear people pray a prayer of repentance to remove any and all hindrances that would prevent their receiving from God. If sin was the cause of the sickness or disease, and after receiving healing that sin is revisited, then the door is opened again for that sickness or disease to come back in. God does not restore people to health in order for them to go back to the sin that caused their sickness and disease in the first place. **Sin revisited opens the door to sickness and disease again, and healing is lost.**

> *John 5:14*
> *14 Later Jesus found him at the temple and said to him, "See, you are well again. Stop sinning or something worse may happen to you."*

While in an auditorium filled with believers, there is a corporate faith at work. Many believers, who are healed, return home to an environment where they will receive little or no encouragement, to continue to claim and declare their healing. Sooner or later, circumstances will occur, statements will be made, all of which will generate doubt and erode the faith, that claimed the healing and declared it to be a reality. **Doubt creeps in which kills the faith, resulting in the loss of healing.**

86

Matt 14:28-31
28 "Lord, if it's you," Peter replied, "tell me to come to you on the water."
29 "Come," he said. Then Peter got down out of the boat, walked on the water and came toward Jesus.
30 But when he saw the wind, he was afraid and, beginning to sink, cried out, "Lord, save me!"
31 Immediately Jesus reached out his hand and caught him. "You of little faith," he said, "why did you doubt?"

The distractions of family, work, and plain everyday living can quickly interfere with the focus of the believer. Time is such a precious commodity, and when the demands placed on us far exceed what is available, something or someone always suffers. In the case of we believers, it always seems that prayer time and time in the word, are the first areas to go. The spiritual chain of command is critical to maintaining a healing. Let me clarify this by saying that while God heals unconditionally, the maintenance of that healing is entirely up to the individual who was healed. If the spiritual aspects in the life of an individual who was healed become non-existent, then doors get opened that allow the enemy back in to steal their health. **Lack of spiritual maintenance can cause a loss of healing.**

Proverbs 4:20-22
20 My son, pay attention to what I say; listen closely to my words.
21 Do not let them out of your sight, keep them within your heart;
22 for they are life to those who find them and health to a man's whole body.

Those of you who have had a life threatening sickness or disease will have no problem relating to what I am about to write. When serious illness falls, your wife/husband, family, neighbours, workmates will have you dead and buried in a matter of minutes. Most people do not realize the power of the tongue. The enemy of our soul, who has writings against us, can use every word spoken about or to us. It is absolutely imperative to claim and declare the healing that God has bestowed, and dedicate it to His glory. **Failure to claim and declare healing to God's glory can result in loss of healing.**

> *Colossians 2:14*
> *14 having canceled the written code, with its regulations, that was against us and that stood opposed to us; he took it away, nailing it to the cross.*

Unfortunately, there are those in the body of Christ who experience nothing more than an emotional experience. Many of these individuals are so hungry for God that they get ahead of the Holy Spirit. They go through all the motions, and can rhyme off the standard textbook list of physical manifestations associated with healing. In all of this they miss the most important aspect of healing, healing happens in the spiritual realm. The physical aspects of healing happen after the work is done in the spiritual realm. The word instructs us not to go by feelings or to look to our symptoms; we are to go by faith and by faith alone, and to speak it out as though it already were.

Chapter 11

The Laying On Of Hands

In the last chapter of the book of Mark, we find recorded what has come to be known as the Great Commission. The word commission means:- giving of authority to a person to perform a given task. Jesus gave His disciples, and we His church, the authority to fulfill the tasks listed in Mark 16: 15-20.

Mark 16:15-20
15 He said to them, "Go into all the world and preach the good news to all creation.
16 Whoever believes and is baptized will be saved, but whoever does not believe will be condemned.
17 And these signs will accompany those who believe: In my name they will drive out demons; they will speak in new tongues;
18 they will pick up snakes with their hands; and when they drink deadly poison, it will not hurt them at all; they will place their hands on sick people, and they will get well."
19 After the Lord Jesus had spoken to them, he was taken up into heaven and he sat at the right hand of God.

20 Then the disciples went out and preached everywhere, and the Lord worked with them and confirmed his word by the signs that accompanied it.

"And these signs will accompany those who believe"…if this statement doesn't excite you, nothing will. "In my name"…in the name of Jesus, we have been given the authority to place hands on sick people and they will get well. The laying on of hands is part of the doctrine of the new covenant, the doctrine of Christ, as detailed in Hebrews 6:1. As such, it is a principle, a fundamental truth, demonstrated, practised and taught, by Jesus Himself.

The laying on of hands is not a practice unique to the New Testament; it was also a common practice in Old Testament times. The fact is, that the practice of the laying on of hands is well documented in the Jewish tradition. A father would place his right hand on the head of his first-born son while imparting his blessing on him. It was part of the formality that established the right of inheritance through the oldest son. In Genesis 48:14, we read how Joseph brought his two sons to his father, Jacob, to receive this very blessing.

In Exodus 29, we are told how Aaron and his sons were consecrated as God's priests. They were instructed to place their hands on the heads of two rams and a bullock, prior to the animals being sacrificed. In these scriptures, the Sins of the Aaron and his sons were transferred by faith to the sacrifice. The important point here is, that sin, was transferred by the laying on of hands. This is a warning to all, be careful who lays hands on you. Just as the sins of the people of Israel were transferred to the animals, you and I can receive spiritual baggage from those who are praying for us. This is why many ministries tightly control their prayer ministry teams, and only certain individuals are allowed to pray for others.

Because of his lack of trust in God, at the waters of Meribah, God said to Moses that he would not be allowed to enter into the Promised Land. Moses then asked God to appoint a new leader for the people, and God chose Joshua. God instructed Moses to have

Joshua stand before Eleazar and the assembly, where Moses would lay hands on Joshua to commission him.

Numbers 27:18
18 So the LORD said to Moses, "Take Joshua son of Nun, a man in whom is the spirit, and lay your hand on him.

In obedience to God, Moses did as he was asked and imparted to Joshua, everything that he had. In Deuteronomy 34, we read that Moses imparted to Joshua the blessing, the inheritance of his power, the spirit if wisdom, by the laying on of hands. So, just as the bad can be transferred, so can the good.

The healing ministry of Jesus included many occurrences involving the laying on of hands. Jairus, a ruler of the synagogue, came to Jesus because his daughter was dying. He was very specific in his request, he asked that Jesus would come and put His hands on her, so that she would be healed and live. Because of his position in the synagogue, Jairus obviously knew what was recorded in the Tora. He knew and accepted the validity of the laying on of hands. He had no doubt seen the ministry of Jesus in action, and knew that when Jesus healed, that it was quite common for Him to lay His hands on the sick.

Mark 5:23
23 and pleaded earnestly with him, "My little daughter is dying. Please come and put your hands on her so that she will be healed and live."

When Jesus came to His hometown of Nazareth, He was not received as the anointed of God. They still considered Him as the son of the carpenter, whose mother, brothers and sisters were still living there. He did very little except lay hands on a few sick people.

Mark 6:5
5 He could not do any miracles there, except lay his hands on a few sick people and heal them.

91

After leaving the synagogue in Capernaum, Jesus went to the house of Simon. After healing Simon's mother-in-law of a fever, she waited on them. Later that evening, the people brought their sick so that Jesus could lay hands on them.

> *Luke 4:40*
> *40 When the sun was setting, the people brought to Jesus all who had various kinds of sickness, and laying his hands on each one, he healed them.*

When Saul was struck blind while on the road to Damascus, Jesus told him to go into the city where he would be told what to do. For three days he was blind, during which time he was given a vision. He saw in his vision a man called Ananius, who would come and place hands on him, so that he would regain his sight. The Lord also spoke to Ananius in a vision, telling him that he was to seek out Saul of Tarsus, and lay hands on him so that his sight would be restored.

> *Acts 9:12*
> *12 In a vision he has seen a man named Ananias come and place his hands on him to restore his sight."*

The man who once hated and persecuted the Christians, became the Apostle Paul, Christianity's greatest ambassador. In time, he too was taken prisoner and was sent to Rome. On route, he was shipwrecked on the island of Malta. There in the home of Publius, he layed hands on the father of Publius, and healed him.

> *Acts 28:8*
> *8 His father was sick in bed, suffering from fever and dysentery. Paul went in to see him and, after prayer, placed his hands on him and healed him.*

We believers have all been given access to this wonderful and precious gift of being able to pray for the healing of others. We are the Lords hands on earth, and He cannot do what He sees the Father do, if we don't get involved. If we do not exercise this doctrine of laying on or placing on of hands, we will be responsible for some people not receiving healing. The Apostle Paul gave some sound advice to Timothy, be an example for the believers, hold fast to the teaching, and do not neglect your gift. Just like Timothy, we must not neglect the gift that Jesus has given us; we must use it for the relief of those who are in sickness and disease, and to bring glory to the Father.

Through the doctrine of the laying on of hands, God's power is transmitted by faith through the minister to the seeker. The laying on or placing on of hands for healing, works for everyone who believes. It worked for Jesus because He did what He saw the Father doing. It works for us because we claim it in Jesus name. Just as Jesus worked with His disciples and confirmed His word with signs and wonders, He will do the same for you and I. We should expect no less of our Lord and Saviour, because He is the same yesterday, today and forever.

Chapter 12

Questions And Answers

These questions, are the seven most asked questions about healing. They are questions that have been asked by both believers and non-believers.

Q: Are sickness and disease always caused by Sin?
A: No.

- All through the Old Testament, the scripture places emphasis on sickness being a direct result of sin. The fall of man, brought about by sin, removed man from divine health.

  Deuteronomy 28:15
  15 However, if you do not obey the LORD your God and do not carefully follow all his commands and decrees I am giving you today, all these curses will come upon you and overtake you:

- The New Testament scripture places emphasis on the healing power of Jesus overcoming the works of the enemy.

Acts 10:38
38 how God anointed Jesus of Nazareth with the Holy Spirit and power and how he went around doing good and healing all who were under the power of the devil, because God was with him.

- When Jesus healed the lame man at the pool of Bethesda, He stated in verse fourteen that sin was the cause.

John 5:14
14 Later Jesus found him at the temple and said to him, "See, you are well again. Stop sinning or something worse may happen to you."

- When Jesus healed the blind man in John chapter nine, He told the disciples that the sickness was not the result of sin.

John 9:3
3 "Neither this man nor his parents sinned," said Jesus, "but this happened so that the work of God might be displayed in his life.

Q: Are sickness and disease from God?
A: No.

- It is God's nature to heal, not to place sickness and disease on us. The belief that some have, that God teaches us through sickness, is totally wrong.

- Sickness and disease do not bring glory to God. We as Christians, cannot profess to be free and have a more abundant life while walking in sickness and disease.

- Sickness can certainly draw the believer closer to God, which in turn can cause the believer to deal with the root cause of the sickness, rather than deal with what the sickness has done.

Romans 2:4
4 Or do you show contempt for the riches of his kindness, tolerance and patience, not realizing that God's kindness leads you toward repentance?

Q: Does every healing happen immediately?
A: No.

- While most healings recorded in the New Testament happened immediately, there was an occasion when Jesus had to pray twice for a blind man.

Mark 8:23-25
23 He took the blind man by the hand and led him outside the village. When he had spit on the man's eyes and put his hands on him, Jesus asked, "Do you see anything?"
24 He looked up and said, "I see people; they look like trees walking around.
25 Once more Jesus put his hands on the man's eyes. Then his eyes were opened, his sight was restored, and he saw everything clearly.

- Sometimes physical healing is progressive because emotional and spiritual issues have to be dealt with **first**.

James 5:14-16
14 Is any one of you sick? He should call the elders of the church to pray over him and anoint him with oil in the name of the Lord.
15 And the prayer offered in faith will make the sick person well; the Lord will raise him up. If he has sinned, he will be forgiven.
16 Therefore confess your sins to each other and pray for each other so that you may be healed. The prayer of a righteous man is powerful and effective.

Q: Does everyone get healed?
A: No.

- In the New Testament, scripture tells us the Jesus healed all who came to Him.

  Matthew 4:24
  24 News about him spread all over Syria, and people brought to him all who were ill with various diseases, those suffering severe pain, the demon-possessed, those having seizures, and the paralyzed, and he healed them.

- When Jesus healed the lame man at the pool of Bethesda, He only healed one of many who were situated around the pool. We must not forget that Jesus does only what He sees the Father doing. While it is our hope, our desire that everyone prayed for be healed, not all will be healed.

Q: Why are some believers not healed?
A: Generally, because they have issues that need to be dealt with before God can deal with them

- In the New Testament writings, there were a number of individuals that were walking in sickness. The Apostle Paul had an eye affliction.

  Galatians 4:13-15
  13 you know, it was because of an illness that I first preached the gospel to you.
  14 Even though my illness was a trial to you, you did not treat me with contempt or scorn. Instead, you welcomed me as if I were an angel of God, as if I were Christ Jesus himself.
  15 What has happened to all your joy? I can testify that, if you could have done so, you would have torn out your eyes and given them to me.

Paul's protégé Timothy had persistent stomach problems.

1 Timothy 5:23
23 Stop drinking only water, and use a little wine because of your stomach and your frequent illnesses.

- If you are required to pray with someone who has not received healing, determine what is preventing the flow of the Holy Spirit. Perhaps the individual may need to repent of something said, done or thought. Maybe there is unbelief, lack of faith, or just plain resistance to the moving of God. It is even possible that they have embraced their sickness or disease because of the attention that it brings. Just like the lame man at the pool of Bethesda, Jesus asked him if he wanted to be healed.

John 5:6
6 When Jesus saw him lying there and learned that he had been in this condition for a long time, he asked him, "Do you want to get well?"

Q: Is it lack of faith for a believer to use medicine?
A: No.

- Jesus and His disciples frequently used oil as an ingredient to the healing process.

Mark 6:13
13 They drove out many demons and anointed many sick people with oil and healed them.

- They also used spittle as an ingredient to the healing process.

John 9:6
6 Having said this, he spit on the ground, made some mud with the saliva, and put it on the man's eyes.

- The Apostle Paul encouraged Timothy to use a little wine for medicinal purposes, because Timothy had an ongoing problem with his stomach. While God is the true source of healing, the truth remains that He can use various means to bring about healing. Medicine is definitely one of his ways of doing just that.

1 Timothy 5:23
23 Stop drinking only water, and use a little wine because of your stomach and your frequent illnesses.

Q: Does sickness have to be to the death?
A: No.

- Every believer knows that sooner or later, preferably later, we all will experience physical death. While we cannot control when God decides to take us home, we do not have to die before our time. Scripture says that we do not have to die from sin, sickness, and judgement.

Hebrews 9:27
27 Just as man is destined to die once, and after that to face judgment,

- Sickness doesn't have to be to the death, because Jesus has control over death, and that control has been given to us believers. Lazarus had been dead for four days before Jesus raised him up and restored him completely. If the death of a believer is imminent, for whatever cause, we must minister comfort and peace to the dying. However, if the Holy Spirit leads us to continue to pray for healing, then we must do just that.

We, who regularly pray for the sick, cannot allow ourselves to be distracted by what we hear or see in the natural. Healing takes place in the spiritual realm before it is manifested in the natural or physical realm.

Epilogue

God never intended for mankind to walk in anything other than divine health. When sin brought about mans removal from divine health, God provided an avenue of relief through divine healing. He then sent His Son Jesus to restore His authority over the earth, and to restore man's relationship with Him. In our new relationship with God, our focus should be to live a Christ centred life, a life that will maintain divine health.

Our mission is to fulfill God's plan and purpose for our lives. To that end, we have been commissioned and equipped with everything that we need, to do His work on earth. We have been given the freedom and right to exercise God's miraculous power to work miracles, including miracles of healing. We are to walk by faith and not by sight, believing for that which we cannot yet see.

It is important to remember that when we pray for the healing of others, we are not responsible for the results. The results will be dependant on the individual, and on what God's will, plan and purpose is for their life. Rather than heal the physical ailment that was prayed for, God may choose to heal an emotional or spiritual hurt that is of greater consequence to the individual.

Recently, after a lengthy battle with cancer, a Christian brother of mine went to be with the Lord. Much prayer had gone up on his behalf and the body of the church believed for his healing. The physical healing that was expected, that was believed for, was not forthcoming. Instead, the Lord chose to take him home where he was totally healed, made whole, in the very presence of God.

Why did God not heal my Christian brother here on earth? I don't know why, but this I do know, that when we don't have all the answers, when we do not understand, all we can do is trust. We are to be obedient to the leading of the Holy Spirit, and pray for those in need of healing. When the healing is not manifested, when things go from bad to worse, we are to dig in our heels and continue believing and trusting. When it's all said and done, it's all about Faith, it's Faith that counts.

We have the power of the anointing and the authority of relationship. When this is activated by faith and in obedience to the Spirit, the healing anointing flows. We must ensure that we always maintain a submissive attitude, having authority yet being under authority. We must have a servant's heart and be faithful and diligent in what God has commissioned us to do. If we do all of these things, God will use us mightily in His Kingdom.

Now that you have completed the reading this book, I invite you to pray the following prayer. It is a prayer of empowerment to all who speak it forth. I have already agreed with all who pray, that God will empower you and use you mightily to heal those in need.

"Father, In the name of Jesus, I ask you to cleanse me, sanctify me, and make me whole in your sight. Father, I ask you to prepare me for the work of your Kingdom. Father, increase my faith and encourage my obedience to your word. Fill me with your Holy Spirit and empower me with your anointing for healing. Father, use me to minister to those who have fallen victim to sickness and disease. Father, work with me, and confirm your word with signs and wonders. Use me mightily in Jesus' name. Father, I thank you for the privilege of being your child, and I give you all the Praise, all the Honour, and all the Glory, in Jesus' name. Amen."

MISSION STATEMENT

Isaiah 61:1
1 The Spirit of the Sovereign LORD is on me,
because the LORD has anointed me to preach
good news to the poor. He has sent me to bind
up the brokenhearted, to proclaim freedom for
the captives and release from darkness for the
prisoners,

In addition to a full time Counselling, Healing, and Deliverance Ministry, Rev. Bob and Sharon Holburn conduct seminars on Healing, Spiritual Gifts, and Motivational Gifts.

If you would like more information about their Ministry, please write: -

Robert Holburn Ministries
13 Twigg Drive
Ajax, Ontario
Canada
L1Z 1G4

e-mail at <u>bobsharonrhm@aol.com</u>

Distributed in Canada by:

131 Cordite Road
Winnipeg, MB R3W 1S1

Phone: (800) 665-1468
Fax: (800) 352-9272
E-mail: orderdesk@wordalive.ca
Website: www.wordalive.ca

Printed in the United States
4412